GW01311244

ISBN-13: 978-1985295025

ISBN-10:1985295024

Funny Irish Phrases

Brendan Moffet

A little collecton of auld jokes and phrases. Sure were only having a laugh! Offensive and at times vulgar.

"You can't get feathers off a plucked Chicken"

When your back is to the wall, or when there is no more money left in the kitty.

"They'd go through you like a short cut"

A person of terse personality that is impolite.

"If there was work on the bed he'd sleep on the floor"

A work-shy or lazy person.

"It's grows on work-time it gets cut on work time"

Referring the hair on ones head. It is permittable for a gentleman to get a haircut while on the clock.

"If you're lucky enough to be Irish...

You're lucky enough!"

"Time for Tae"

'Tae' as in 'Tea'. No, not a spelling error. It is fashionable to say 'Time for Tae' especially while in work or on-the-job.

"You made a hames of it"

To mess something up or not complete a task correctly. To put it on the wrong way.

"I gave her the How's your father"

A very cheeky way of saying that a romantic deed is done.

"Sound as a bell"

A expression that signifies a person is helpful, friendly and of genuine character.

"Scuttered"

When a person is highly intoxicated. Many other terms such as "Blotto", "in the horrors" and "twisted".

"She's not fit for soft ground"

A lady that is robust and rotund. (Typically expressed in private)

"Throw your number in there please"

When entering a pin number at a cashier desk. Throw been the adapted use if the verb 'to throw'.

"Do you want your go?"

Used to challenge someone to a fight!

"I loves me County"

The use of 'me' is not a typo or spelling mistake. The use 'me' in place of 'my' signifies a great deal of affection for ones home county.

"The jacks"

Referring to the Restroom or toilet.

"He'd get a week out of a chicken"

A phrase used to illustrate when a person is careful with money and lacking generosity.

"A cute cunt"

Definiately not a compliment. It can be used to describe a mean (financially) person or someone who is sneaky.

"I'm gunna head on"

As in "head on," which means you're going to leave.

"A head like a jockeys bollocks"

Referring to the state of being severely hungover where a persons physical appearance is far from presentable.

"Wipe that puss off your face"

If someone has a "puss" on them, (frown or scowl) when there is no justified reason. A person that is in bad humor or perhaps moody.

"He was 'polluted"

Intoxicated.

"He's hungry out"

A miser

'Chalk it down'

To express agreement or consensus on a point or topic.
"The price of drink is disgraceful"- Chalk it down lad,
chalk it down."

"He got a fifty last night"

Failure to turn up for an arranged meeting, especially a date 'Dave is furious, he got a fifty.

"There's more than one way to skin a chat. I just don't like the way you skin yours"

To highlight a difference in viewpoint or opinion.

"Strain the spuds"

To go to the toilet to urinate

"Doing a line"

This does not refer to abuse of substances. If one is "doing a line" with someone it means the are dating or in a relationship.

"A BIFFO"

A beautiful intelligent female from Offaly (County Offaly, Ireland)

"Now were sucking Diesel"

When times are good are you come in to good fortune.

"A drop of scald"

A nice hot cup of tea.

"A drop of scald"

A nice hot cup of tea.

"I'd suck farts from her arse"

When you like a lady of exceptional beauty.

"True friends stab you in the front"

Oscar Wilde.

"Some cause happiness wherever they go; others whenever they go."

Oscar Wilde.

"Rome wasn't built in A.D."

Flann O'Brien

'Away with the fairies'

Someone who is crazy or not been realistic.

"The older the fiddle the sweeter the tune"

When appreciating the beauty of an older man or woman.

"Let sleeping dogs lie"

Some things are best left unsaid.

"Throw shapes"

To dance energetically.

"Are You Okay?"

The typical greeting of the sales assistant or bartender. Nothing to do with health or well-being. The phrase translates as "I am ready to serve you

"Hole in the Wall"

An ATM or bank machine.

"A Nod Is As Good As A Wink To A Blind Horse"

When you agree with someone expressing a point in a subtle way. Normally related to something illegal or sexual in nature. "Say no more" – I understand.

"An Old Broom Knows The Dirty Corners Best"

You cant put an old head on young shoulders. Experience has a value.

"Get the finger out"

To get motivated or stop been lazy.

"Throwing a sausage down O'Connell Street"

When a lady is renowned for her many dates and the potential impact therein.

"Running around like a headless chicken"

When you are struggling to complete something or are in a desperate situation.

"On the duck"

To avoid going to classes (usually in high school). "On the hop" is also popular in certain parts of Ireland.

Printed in Great Britain
by Amazon

30194957R00020